MOKSHA PADAM

MOKSHA PADAM

Delve Into Your Inner Self

ROOPA V RAJAN

ISBN 13: 978-93-5530-156-7
ISBN 10: 93-5530-156-1

Printed in India and published by BUUKS.

TABLE OF CONTENTS

GRATITUDE

I express my humble obeisance to all my gurus. All glory to Saint Gyandev, Sai Baba and my living Sadhguru Dattatreya Siva Baba (Babaji).

Please accept my deep gratitude for your guidance and encouragement that made it possible for us to develop this new form of the *Moksha Padam* board game.

Playing this game reveals many hidden dimensions within our subconscious mind. Delving deeper into it revealed to me the content of my subconscious and helped me release many fears, phobias, and deep-rooted sorrows. The game also showed me effective remedies to defuse problems and ease our suffering.

Every square has some wisdom to offer. Each square takes us one step deeper into the subconscious. It was amazing for me to know that playing this game in the two-hour window of time before sunset takes one into deeper realms.

Gratitude to all *sadhgurus* for this incredible privilege. Even though the game was known for centuries, you have decided that it needs to come out in a new form. I beseech you to show the light of divine love to everyone and allow them to be blessed by *siddhas* and sadhgurus.

I express my deepest gratitude for the pearls of wisdom you are giving us. With the blessings of sadhgurus and siddhas, may this board game reach every household.

ACKNOWLEDGEMENT

I thank Ram for taking time out to edit this book. I appreciate and thank him for his dedication to publishing this. I extend my gratitude to Manjula Premkumar for creating the beautiful handmade illustrations for this board. I would like to thank Dr. Latha for correcting the Sanskrit words and providing the script for them.

I sincerely thank my husband, Varadarajan, and my adorable daughters, Gargi and Sindhu, for their love, encouragement and support.

ABOUT THE GAME

*M*oksha Padam* is a board game believed to have been created by the 13th-century Indian mystic, saint and poet Gyan Dev to teach Hindu *dharma* and values to children. Certain historical references indicate the game could have originated in the second century BC. This board contains 72 squares, each of which represents a state of consciousness.

The ladders in the game represent virtues while the snakes indicate vices. The fundamental lesson of the game continues to be the same – good deeds take us to a higher dimension and ignorant actions take us into a constant cycle of negativity.

The ladders starting from squares that denote good qualities lead to various heavens (*Kailasa*, *Vaikuntha* and *Brahma loka*) and are nothing but higher states of consciousness. Conversely, each snake's head is there to heal a state of ignorance within us.

PURPOSE OF THE GAME

TO GROW AND PROSPER

This game serves a dual purpose – entertainment and understanding the subconscious mind. In addition, playing this game can help us deeply integrate cosmic principles and values, enabling us to live a more conscious life and achieve our desires without strife.

The final goal is always completion and transition into a new 'Heaven on Earth' where everything is easily accessible, and there is no suffering.

Each square in the game represents a value or vice in our subconscious mind. As we move through the squares in the game, the descriptions in this book will help you delve deeper into your inner self. Irrespective of whether you progress higher with a ladder or go down the rows with a snake, playing this game enables you to resolve issues and defuse unhealthy patterns in your life.

It is human nature to want more from life. So, even if we are happy with what we have now, it is our nature to expand our consciousness. This game will assist you in achieving your desires with grace and making your experience on Earth a more fulfilling one.

HOW TO PLAY THE GAME

WHAT YOU NEED

* The *Moksha Padam* board
* One die
* Player piece
* *Moksha Padam* guidebook

You can play this game as a single player or together with others. Each player puts their piece on the first square that says *uthpathi* (beginning). Roll your die and according to the number shown on the die, move your piece forward on the board. For example, if you roll a 5, you will move your piece five squares.

The players will move their pieces from left to right, starting from *uthpathi* (1) and then right to left on the next row. Following the order of numbers, you will move left to right and right to left alternately on each row.

If you land at the bottom of a ladder, you can move up to the top of the ladder. If you land on top of a snake, you must go down to the bottom of the snake.

As you land on each square, refer to the description of the square in the *Moksha Padam* guidebook to understand the deeper subconscious meaning of that square. Contemplate how this may relate to your life journey, desires and challenges.

There is no winner in this game. The progress of your game reflects the journey of your life.

When you come to a ladder, you skip steps to go far ahead in the game. The ladders are symbols of rapid evolution. When you come to a snake, you fall back to one of the lower squares in the game. The snakes represent flaws that impede your progress, whether material or spiritual.

Further to the insights in the guidebook, you can also get readings from Roopaji that will provide answers to your questions and issues. Based on your questions and your movement through the squares of the board game, Roopaji will give you a greater intuitive understanding of your problems, as well as solutions and remedies to overcome blocks that impede your material or spiritual expansion and evolution. To get a full reading, please get in touch with Roopaji: roopavrajan@gmail.com

DOWNLOADING THE BOARD GAME AND INSTRUCTIONS FOR PRINTING

You can download a high-resolution image of the board game on the link below.

https://qrco.de/bd4IRG

You can print the board game either on a flex board, cardboard, cloth or vinyl. Your local printing shop will be able to give different options for printing.

THE MOST AUSPICIOUS TIME TO PLAY THE GAME

Playing this game at any time of the day will help you release unhealthy karmic patterns. However, the most auspicious time to play this game is the two-hour window before sunset in any time zone. The energies during this time are most conducive to releasing unwholesome thoughts, emotions and beliefs that limit the expansion of your consciousness.

SQUARES OF MOKSHA PADAM BOARD GAME 1–72

1. *UTHPATHI* (BEGINNING)

Everything in life has to begin somewhere. Desire is the beginning of the process of creation. To create and manifest anything, you need a clear desire. Visualising your desire with the right emotions is vital for creating what you want. This propels your mind in the right direction. Good health, happiness, security, peace of mind and prosperity are expressions of authentic desire.

2. *MAYA* (ILLUSION)

Maya is denoted as an illusion. The illusion of energy is created within our *muladhara* (root chakra at the base of the spine) flowing towards the *ajna* or third eye near the eyebrow. This energy flowing is simply the supreme consciousness, the eternal force. At any given time, *maya* can create many states of consciousness without ceasing to be an unlimited force.

3. *KRODHA* (FURY, WRATH, RAGE AND INDIGNATION)

Krodha is the offspring of *kama* (desire). When a desire is not realised, it can produce *krodha*. It can bind a person to low self-esteem. This internal vibration can hamper the goals and aspirations of an individual. We generally allow challenging experiences to rule us by holding on to them. The power of *sankalpa* (intention) alone is enough to change any situation.

The easiest way to defuse the enemies of the mind is to propitiate Lord Ganesha, the elephant-headed God:

Pray to *Lambodara* Ganesha (pot-bellied Ganesha) to remove *krodha* caused by Mars.

4. *LOBHA* (GREED OR AVARICE)

Desires keep changing as one's outlook and values change. Clarity of mind is essential to hold on to a particular goal. When we keep changing the goal, it reverses the energy flow of manifestation, resulting in confusion. Whenever there is negative vibration within ourselves, it causes the creative energy to fall back into the *muladhara*. Place an intention and do inner work to get rid of *lobha*.

Pray to *Gajanana* Ganesha (elephant-faced Ganesha) for removing lobha caused by Saturn.

5. *BHU LOKA* (THE EARTH PLANE)

Bhu loka is the plane of earthly existence, where we have come to progress in our evolution. Earth is the only dimension where we can see and perceive things in three-dimensional form. The earth plane also holds the energy of love. You cannot complete any action on this dimension without love and determination. The energy of love gives you clarity of mind.

6. *MOHA* (CRAVING)

KETU

The very nature of consciousness is to observe, feel and desire. But when desire becomes obsessive, we will be thrown out of balance and it becomes craving. Yet, one should not deny desire because it is an integral part of consciousness. What we need to do is identify unhealthy and inauthentic cravings to redirect our desire towards more wholesome ends. This becomes easier when we can conncct to something bigger than our limited self. This will ease the distortions caused by craving.

7. *MADA* (TRANSLATED AS FALSE EGO, PRIDE AND INTOXICATION)

RAHU

Mada is a major obstacle to manifestation. When consumed by *mada*, our navel chakra can get disconnected from source energy. This will make one confused and ungrounded, which can disrupt the creative process. All experiences, events, conditions and actions are the reactions of the subconscious mind to thoughts within. Our innermost beliefs that lie deep within the subconscious mind manifest outwardly. Identifying and removing false beliefs, opinions, superstitions and fears can help us remove obstacles to manifestation.

Pray to *Dhumravarna* Ganesha (ash-coloured Ganesha) for overcoming *mada* caused by Rahu.

8. *TRISHNA* (THIRST)

Trishna is necessary for a fulfilling experience on the earth plane. By sowing thoughts of peace, happiness, right action, goodwill and prosperity in the garden of your mind, you will reap a glorious harvest on the earth plane.

9. *KAMA* (LUST)

Venus

Kama is one of the essential goals of human life. When pursued without sacrificing the other three goals of *dharma*, *artha* and *moksha*, *kama* is a healthy pursuit. Our subconscious mind holds all kinds of thoughts and emotions. It is essential to have a clear mind and consistent thoughts to manifest any desire. By channelling the right thoughts and using the power of the subconscious, you can resolve any problem or difficulty. When you channel your innate power, you are consciously cooperating with the cosmic law of omnipotence. An agitated mind can obstruct breathing, resulting in a weakening of the *chandranadi* (left nostril).

Pray to *Vikata* Ganesha (large-toothed Ganesha) to defuse lower forms of *kama* caused by Venus, which can create greed and anger.

10. *TAPASYA* (AUSTERITIES)

Tapasya refers to a disciplined endeavour to achieve a goal. *Tapasya* involving self-discipline, rigorous training and virtuous living can help activate special inner powers. Any meditation practice or contemplation cleanses the body and mind of destructive habit patterns. Changing habitual thoughts and the emotions associated with them causes great emotional turmoil. A powerful inertia causes us to stay in these unwanted patterns. This can cause suffering. *Tapasya* can help you remove the deeper cause of discord, confusion, lack and limitation.

11. *GANDHARVA LOKA* (PLANE OF CELESTIAL SINGERS AND MUSICIANS)

Gandharva loka is a plane where the Gandharvas, a class of celestial singers, musicians and dancers live. They have the ability to receive nectar and infuse it into some unique plants, giving them special healing capacities. Gandharvas themselves are great healers too. They receive messages from divine sources and deliver them to human beings. Every thought of ours has structure, colour, meaning and a corresponding sound pattern. Sound, music and dance have a special impact on our physical and mental health.

12. *IRSHYA* (ENVY)

Irshya or envy is a destructive emotion that can affect us mentally and physically. When there is envy in our minds, we feel hostile, resentful, angry and irritable. Envy is also related to depression, anxiety, prejudice and unhappiness. This mental state can impact one's health. *Irshya* is a highly agitated state of mind that makes you crave things others possess. Tendencies of *irshya* can be released systematically by identifying and acknowledging them.

Pray to *Vakratunda* Ganesha (curved-trunk Ganesha) for removing *matsarya* and *irshya* caused by Mercury.

13. *ANTARIKSH* (A PLANE BETWEEN BHU LOKA AND BHUVAR LOKA)

Moon

Each thought or idea in your conscious mind brings a response from the subconscious. As soon as your subconscious accepts an idea, it proceeds to realise it. It uses all the knowledge we have gathered in our various lifetimes to actualise the idea. We can draw infinite power, energy and wisdom from within. It lines up all the laws of nature to get its way, often-times bringing immediate solutions.

14. *BHUVAR LOKA* – THE SECOND DIMENSION ABOVE THE EARTH PLANE

Bhuvar loka is a plane that represents the ability of our subjective mind to perceive without sense organs. The subjective mind is clairvoyant and clairaudient. This mental faculty enables one to leave the body, travel to distant lands and bring back accurate information. A subjective mind is intuitive and can read others' thoughts.

15. *NAG LOKA* (THE PLANE OF SNAKES)

You can defuse fear, worry and other destructive thought forms by recognising the omnipotence of the subconscious mind. The omnipotent mind enables us to experience freedom, happiness and perfect health. Having immense faith in our creative power and connection to our source can bring us the highest freedom and happiness.

16. *DVESHA* (GRUDGE)

Dvesha is a feeling of deep-seated resentment towards people and situations. Recalling a past event and the negative emotions associated with them can create grudges and unwanted stress. Rushing to forgive isn't good either, as it makes you deny or suppress emotions.

Finding out why you are holding on to a grudge can make it easier for you to let go. The easiest way to let go of a grudge is to look at it from a different perspective. This allows you to accept the situation or let it go.

Being hurt by people, particularly someone you love and trust, can cause anger, sadness and confusion. If you dwell too much on hurtful events, feelings of vengeance and hostility can consume you. Forgive yourself and others.

17. *DAYA* (COMPASSION)

Daya is a much deeper emotion than sympathy. It also involves empathy, which allows people to build social connections. By understanding what people are thinking and feeling, *daya* enables one to respond appropriately in any social situation.

Empathising with others helps to regulate our own emotions and inculcate a helpful mindset. It is one of the important building blocks of effective social interaction. When a person shows compassion, it takes them to a higher dimension.

18. *HARSHA* (HAPPINESS)

Happiness is a state of mind characterised by joy, satisfaction, contentment and fulfilment. External situations can cause happiness within a person, but it is essentially defined and generated internally. Brain chemicals are the physical markers of happiness. Science has discovered that the feeling of happiness is created by four primary brain chemicals – dopamine, oxytocin, serotonin and endorphin (DOSE). Happy and joyous people feel confident and are not too worried about what others think about them. Happiness can also empower you to be open and honest.

19. *KARMA* (ACTION)

All deep thoughts will bear fruit either now or in the future. *Karma* is nothing but the consequence of a person's thoughts, feelings and actions. Karma is not a fatalistic concept. It is essentially the destiny we have created using our free will, consciously or unconsciously. To be aware of what kind of karma we are creating now, we need to stay constantly alert.

20. *DAAN* (CHARITY)

Daan is the practice of giving something we consider our own to people who are in need. Charity is always done without expecting anything in return. *Daan* can be an act of donation to larger projects like buildings, schools or hospitals. It could also involve creating public facilities or planting trees. Charity expands the subconscious mind and helps to neutralise enemies and eliminate vices.

21. *SAMMAN* (RESPECT)

Respect means accepting people as they are, even when they're different from you or you don't agree with them. Respect in any relationship builds trust, safety and well-being. Listening patiently, being considerate, and acknowledging people with appropriate words are key to respecting them. Responding to someone's mistakes with kindness and honouring their physical boundaries are some other ways in which we can express respect. Respect is all about acknowledging our worth and that of others. When we do not express respect, we're not in the flow of life.

22. *DHARMA* (THE RIGHT PATH)

Dharma means 'right way of living' and 'path of righteousness'. The meaning of the word depends on the context. Truth is the highest *dharma* and the source of all other virtues. Essentially, it boils down to being compassionate towards all living beings. Unlimited love and joy flow when we're on this path. When *dharma* is established within, all desires are sublimated, and we can gain access to the universal source.

23. *SWARG* (HEAVEN)

Swarg is a state of consciousness that we have the choice of dwelling in. We create heaven when we are in tune with the power of our absolute consciousness. Pain and suffering are not required to inhabit *swarg*. Heaven and hell are choices within us. When we are steeped in this awareness, all our actions are guided by the God within us, who will think, act and speak through us. This is the essence of *swarg*.

24. *DUSANGA* (BAD COMPANY)

Dusanga can destroy confidence. Ill-meaning friends or relatives can cause misery. People who are 'bad company' enjoy the misfortune of others, have control issues and are habitually dishonest. They lack remorse and responsibility and can mislead you. Be aware of people who are not aligned with your energy. Bad company can jeopardise your desires and bring in negativity.

25. *SATSANGA* (GOOD COMPANY)

Communing with people who are aligned with our subtle divine energy will help us purify our thoughts and create new ones that can fulfil our desires. *Satsanga* can help us cultivate good qualities. Good people positively influence others and help them grow and thrive. They generate positive energy and a vibrant auric field, which can also bring wealth and good health.

26. *SHOK* (MOURNING)

Shok is an expression of grief following a loss. You can be in a state of depression and confusion or lose interest in friends and social activities. Brooding over things can create negative vibrations. It makes the mind wallow in the past. Being cheerful, joyful and purposeful can help you break out of the pattern of sadness and regret.

27. *PARAMA DHARMA* (ULTIMATE DHARMA)

Parama dharma is one's 'ultimate duty' that supersedes all other duties. It is our higher duty to humanity and the community. Our *parama dharma* requires us to practise non-violence in speech, action and thought. Reaching this square is a reminder that you have followed your *parama dharma* at some point in your life, thereby accessing higher energies and dimensions.

28. *SWADHARMA* (ONE'S OWN DHARMA)

Swadharma means practising one's individual dharma, which includes one's unique duties and responsibilities with righteousness. Everyone is born with their innate traits, nature and capacities. When we recognise and accept the duties that come with our unique nature, all our actions can be performed effortlessly. This gives us tremendous faith in our ability to realise our desires easily. If there are any hindrances and blockages in the subconscious mind, following our *swadharma* will help us overcome them.

29. *ADHARMA* (LACK OF DHARMA OR RIGHTEOUSNESS)

Adharma simply implies a lack of *dharma*. It is the root of fear and suffering. Unrighteous actions such as lying, cheating, stealing and committing crimes constitute *adharma*. It essentially results from the imbalance of the three *gunas – tamas*, *rajas* and *sattva*. These can be balanced within oneself with true faith in divinity.

30. *UTTAM GATI* (IDEAL TEMPO)

Uttam gati helps us make the right decisions at the right time. It is also linked to the right kind of breathing, which calms the mind and defuses toxic emotions and speech. Practising the right kind of breathing can relieve one from stress and nervousness. Being devoted and sincere to a guru can also lead to *uttam gati*.

31. *SPARDHA* (COMPETITION)

Healthy competition and appreciating others' success can create joy. A competitive spirit stems from a growth mindset and can be used in a positive way to achieve our goals. *Spardha* becomes healthy when it's about enriching oneself. The most productively competitive environments recognise the value of the journey rather than the outcome.

32. *MAHAR LOKA* (PLANE OF CONSCIOUSNESS)

Mahar loka describes the fourth-highest realm or plane of consciousness. Only by releasing low-vibration emotions like unwanted fear, jealousy and hatred can one journey into higher planes of consciousness. From the perspective of consciousness, this plane is the realm of the *anahata chakra* (heart centre), which is associated with love, compassion, empathy and forgiveness. When a person reaches this plane in the subconscious mind, desires are realised with amazing speed.

33. *GANDHA* (FRAGRANCE)

Gandha is the sense of smell, which provides an important aspect of the soul's external experiences. It is a quality of the earth element. Diseases can manifest due to a lack of coordination between the sense organs and sense objects. The sense of smell is one of the factors that determine the quality of our desires and our ability to conceptualise a manifestation.

34. *RASA* (ESSENCE OF TASTE)

Rasa is a quality of the water element. In the physical world, it is understood as taste – manifesting as sweet, sour, salty and so on through our salivary glands. Taste is perceived when something touches the tongue. Salivary glands on each side of our mouth give us the essence of *rasa* and taste. They send important signals to the brain and subconscious mind. The element of taste is an integral part of the manifestation process.

35. *NARAKA* (PLANE BELOW THE EARTH)

Naraka is a plane that is said to lie beneath the earth. Naraka translates loosely as 'abode of darkness'. It is only a temporary location within the mind. When we allow divine light to enter our consciousness, we can release dark thoughts and unwanted thinking that bind us to the 'plane of darkness'.

36. *SPASHTATHA* (CLARITY)

A clear, calm and collected mind brings clarity. The easiest way to get clarity is through meditation and proper breathing. When unwanted thoughts clutter your mind, it is essential to mentally distance yourself from them. Worrying about outcomes and consequences makes one muddle-headed and indecisive. This can create tension and stress. Lack of clarity can make one lose faith. When something is done without faith and trust, it has no value, even if it is sacrifice, charity or austerity.

37. *GYANA* (KNOWLEDGE)

Gyana or the power of knowledge is one of the three main parts of creative cosmic power. The other two are *iccha shakti* (willpower) and *kriya shakti* (the power of action). *Gyana shakti* is also the power to know clearly. When all three powers are in harmony, you can attain any goal.

38. *PRANA* (PLANE OF ENERGY)

Prana is the life force or vital principle that permeates all levels of reality, including inanimate objects. It is the source of all movement in the body. *Prana* regulates our conscious and unconscious bodily functions like breath, digestion, blood flow, elimination, cellular growth and healing. *Prana shakti* manifests in our awareness like a pulse or vibration. It can also be absorbed through pure water. One can absorb the life force of the sun, moon, galaxy or cosmos through water. The *prana* from water is absorbed through the pores of the skin and your eyes.

39. *APANA* (ENERGY OF ELIMINATION)

Elimination is one of the important aspects of life processes. Unwanted thoughts need to be purged. One of the five different pranic energies within the body, *apana* is active in the lower abdominal region. The *apana* energy drives the elimination of waste from the body. When anger, fear and negative thoughts are not purged, *apana* can get disturbed. Dullness, laziness and confusion are manifestations of disturbed *apana vayu*.

40. *VYANA* (ENERGY OF INTEGRATION)

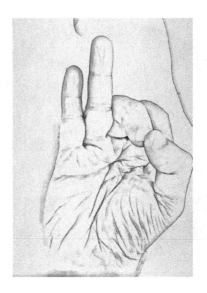

Vyana vayu, also known as 'omnipresent air', helps one to balance the four other *vayus* of the body. This energy of integration governs the movement of *prana* through the *nadis*, keeping them open, clear, clean and functioning properly. Nourishing and expansive, *vyana* governs the movement of *prana* through the *nadis* (the 72,000 energy channels that traverse the body). *Vyana* circulates throughout the body and is responsible for the circulation and distribution of blood, air and nutrients. It provides the building blocks needed for the formation and maintenance of tissues.

41. *JANA LOKA* (PLANE OF CREATIVITY)

Jana loka is a term used to describe the highest plane of the consciousness of creativity. In *jana loka*, thoughts exist in the realm of the *vishuddha chakra* (throat centre), which is associated with inner truth and understanding. If the desires of the *vishuddha chakra* are not met in the current lifetime, they will be manifested in another lifetime.

42. *AGNI* (PURIFICATION BY FIRE)

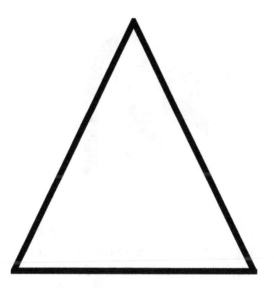

Agni or fire represents immortality. *Agni* is the symbol of life and the soul. It also represents the power of change. Light, heat, colour and energy are merely the outer attributes of *agni*. Inwardly, *agni* impels consciousness and perception and has the power to discriminate. Fire has the power to cleanse excess and unwanted thoughts.

43. *SRISHTI* (CREATION)

Srishti has various meanings including 'whole Earth', 'creation' and 'gift of the cosmic universe'. The universe itself manifests and de-manifests. At the dawn of creation, the whole universe comes into manifestation from *prakriti* (the unmanifest). Belief and trust are important feelings that propel manifestation.

44. *AVIDYA* (INCORRECT KNOWLEDGE)

Incorrect knowledge arises with rigid thoughts, ego, lack of faith and trust. Conceiving right thoughts by weeding out unwanted worthless thoughts is essential for progress. *Avidya* is one of the five illusions involved in the act of creation. *Avidya* arises from *tamas* (darkness).

45. *SUVIDYA* (GOOD KNOWLEDGE)

Suvidya refers to knowledge that lifts the soul. Faith, fortitude and prosperity are all related to *suvidya*. Your knowledge ceases to expand when faith diminishes, even if you are learned and intelligent. To manifest your desires, you need to dive deeper to gain subtle secret knowledge. Being endowed with *suvidya* enables you to bring together the knowledge of what you desire and the right action needed to manifest it.

46. *VIVEKA* (DISCERNMENT)

Viveka can be translated as discernment or correct under-standing. One of the attributes of a true seeker is the ability to differentiate. Patanjali's *Yoga Sutra* explains *viveka* clearly. When the mind and *chitha* are unwavering, *viveka* sets in. When the mind is functioning in a state of *viveka*, there is no room for doubt or misery. When we are in a state of *viveka*, we can experience absolute freedom.

47. *SARASWATI* (RIVER OF KNOWLEDGE)

Human beings are endowed with the powers of speech, wisdom and learning. The four main aspects of the human personality are mind, intellect, alertness and ego. *Saraswati* flows within us in the form of words and sentences. There is an intuitive faculty within us that enables us to understand the truth of any situation. We need to trust this faculty to gain insights.

48. *YAMUNA* (RIVER OF SOLAR ENERGY)

Yamuna symbolises the *pingala nadi*, which flows on the right side of our body. This *nadi* is associated with solar energy. The fear of death is one of the deepest emotions that need to be removed from our subconscious mind. This will liberate us from worrying about outcomes.

49. *GANGA* (RIVER OF PURIFICATION)

Ganga tells us that our thoughts need to be purified. Distorted thoughts can cause mental and bodily ailments. *Ganga* purifies our thoughts, bringing us to a state of completeness in which prosperity consciousness arises. When *Ganga* flows in our consciousness, we lose the fear of life and death. Purification of thoughts automatically clears remnants of past DNA.

50. *TAPO LOKA* (SPHERE OF AUSTERITY)

Tapo loka is a plane of austerities. In this plane, consciousness is untouched by fire. Fire knows which thoughts need to be decimated and which ones need to be retained. In this plane, the subconscious is purified by the fire element.

51. *PRITHVI* (PLANE OF EARTH)

Prithvi is a representation of feminine energy and one of the five elements of the universe, which also includes water, fire, air and space. These elements are the building blocks of the universe. Balancing the five elements helps one maintain good physical and mental health. *Prithvi mudra*, a yogic hand gesture, balances the earth element in the body and relieves fatigue, promotes endurance, boosts self-confidence and increases physical tolerance.

52. *HIMSA* (VIOLENCE)

Violence represents both physical and psychological harm. *Himsa* within our subconscious mind can manifest as prejudice, contempt, physical or psychological assault or abusive words and actions. Even harbouring hateful thoughts is a form of violence. In short, *himsa* represents anything that causes suffering to oneself or others. *Himsa* creates energetic disharmonies within us.

53. *JAL* (WATER)

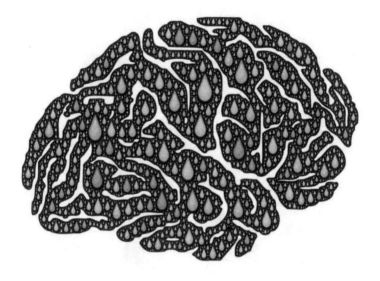

Jal refers to the water element. Water is called 'the elixir of life'. A mere two per cent drop in the body's water content can cause serious dehydration, affecting our short-term memory and ability to focus. Drinking water reduces daytime fatigue and improves memory. Water represents flexibility and flow. Water teaches us to keep flowing, without rigid thoughts and opinions.

54. *BHAKTI* (DEVOTION)

Bhakti or devotion is generated internally when one is ready to surrender unconditionally to the divine source. Devotion can lead us to higher levels of consciousness. *Bhakti* also gives us access to cosmic energy and enables us to experience unconditional love.

55. AHANKAR (EGO)

Ahankar is one of the four parts of the subtle inner organ. The ego plays a vital role in the evolution of our consciousness. Ego is the active function of the mind – it is the doing, thinking function. The ego is an important part of life, as it gives us identity and acts as the activating or initiating force. However, too much selfishness or ego can make us arrogant and self-important. By its nature, the ego doesn't allow consciousness to expand. The ego can be refined by practising humility, which helps one rapidly expand consciousness.

56. *OMKARA* (SOUND OF 'OM')

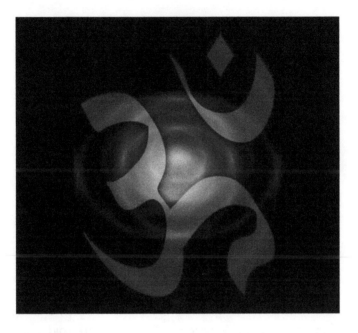

Nada yoga is the science of inner transformation through sound and tone. The entire cosmos is made up of sound vibrations or *nadas*. The vibration of 'Om' is used to treat various spiritual and psychological conditions. *Omkara* helps one energise and increase awareness of the chakras to remove *samskaras* or psychic impressions.

57. *VAYU* (WIND OR AIR)

The element of air represents all kinds of kinetic energy including *prana*, our life energy. When the dark void of *akasha* or sky space is agitated by motion, *vayu* is created in the form of a delicate, light blue-grey energy. The five *prana vayus* include *prana*, *apana*, *samana*, *udana* and *vyana*. Each *vayu* governs a different area of the body. *Prana vayu* is associated with the *anahata* chakra (heart centre). The heart centre governs the intake of *prana* into the lungs while *udana vayu* is associated with *vishudhi* (throat chakra). The vocalisation of thoughts happens in the throat. When there is no fear in the subconscious mind and heart centre, thought energy is harmonious and free flowing and finds a natural articulation.

58. *TEJA* (PLANE OF LIGHT)

Teja symbolises knowledge and wisdom. Everything in the universe is made up of light particles. When we allow cosmic light to enter our being, the atoms inside us vibrate with the speed of cosmic light, removing subconscious malice, violence, lust, envy, injustice, greed, oppression and suffering. According to science, light travels at a speed of 300,000 kilometres per second. Saints and rishis attain things with the speed of light.

59. *SATYA LOKA* (PLANE OF TRUTH)

Satya loka describes the highest plane of consciousness or the highest plane of truth. In the chakra system, the plane of truth is described as the fixed eternal reality and the realm of the *sahasrara* chakra. This is the chakra that connects to divine universal consciousness. Spiritual awareness is nothing but awareness of self and spirit.

60. *SADBUDHI* (WISDOM)

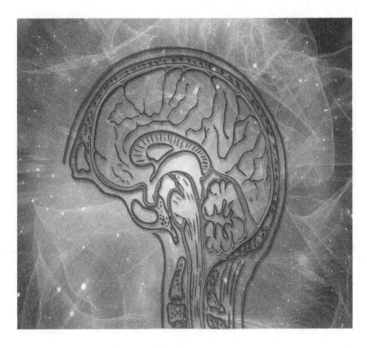

Sadbudhi is the quality of being wise, which brings intelligence in speech and judiciousness in conduct. It refers to the use of discernment and judgement to ascertain what is right. Following *dharma* also brings wisdom. Having true *sadbudhi* is vital in modern society.

61. *DURBUDHI* (LACK OF INTELLIGENCE)

Lack of intelligence in any action manifests as a lack of judiciousness and wisdom. *Durbudhi* causes irresponsible speech, which is in our subconscious mind. It makes one act without clarity and judge things in an egotistical manner. It can bring a person down and compromise his or her integrity.

62. *SUKH* (HAPPINESS OR DELIGHT)

Happiness is an emotional state characterised by feelings of joy, satisfaction, contentment and fulfilment. The main types of happiness relate to pleasure, passion and purpose. Happiness eludes us when we are attached to outcomes. Establishing and building self-esteem is essential to happiness.

63. *TAMAS* (DARKNESS)

Tamas is one of the three tendencies of the human being. It is the quality of inertia, inactivity, dullness or lethargy. *Tamas* manifests because of ignorance. *Tamasic* qualities include disgust, attachment, depression, helplessness, doubt, guilt, shame, boredom, addiction, hurt, sadness, apathy, confusion, grief, dependency and ignorance. In excess, *tamas* creates ignorance, delusion and suffering. *Tamas* can be reduced and balanced by doing meditation, making simple dietary and lifestyle changes, spending time in nature and doing *pranayama*.

64. *PRAKRITHI* (NATURE)

The *Bhagavad Gita* describes *prakriti* as the 'primal motive force'. It is the animating force behind everything in the universe and the very basis of creation. It is also the natural form of anything in manifested form. In *prakriti*, the three *guṇas* or innate qualities of *rajas* (creation), *sattva* (preservation) and *tamas* (destruction) – are in perfect balance. It implies the original state of something or a being. Activating an individual's *prakriti* brings balance and restores one's true nature.

65. *SUKRUTHI* (GOOD DEEDS)

Good deeds are done to fulfil one's duty unselfishly, without concerns of whether they will result in happiness or distress, loss or gain, victory or defeat. *Sukruthi* always gives unlimited joy and expansion of consciousness.

66. *ANANDA LOKA* (PLANE OF BLISS)

Ananda loka is the abode of supreme bliss. In the body, it corresponds to the innermost sheath of the aura, the *anandamaya kosha*, which represents cosmic consciousness. The plane of bliss refers to inner happiness, not the limited happiness resulting from external objects and events. In the plane of bliss, joy and happiness are felt internally without any attachment.

67. *SHIVA LOKA* (PLANE OF SHIVA)

Shiva loka is the world of Shiva. Half of *Shiva loka* is eternally covered with an impenetrable darkness, where not even the slightest trace of light is visible. The other half shines brightly as if lit by a billion moons. This part of *Shiva loka* has an indescribable beauty, which surpasses everything in the worlds below it. This corresponds to our own consciousness, which has both light and darkness.

68. *VAIKUNTH LOKA* (PLANE OF VISHNU)

Vaikuntha loka is the world of the Lord of Creation or the archetype, Vishnu. *Vaikuntha* is the final frontier when it comes to wealth, royalty, magnificence and grandeur. *Vaikuntha* is filled with cities of the most extraordinary grandeur. This is the most opulent, extravagant and affluent plane of consciousness. You do not experience any anxiety or duality in this plane. The name of this plane is made up of two parts – *Vai* meaning 'no' and *kunta* meaning 'death'.

69. *BRAHMA LOKA* (HIGHEST ABODES OF CREATION)

Brahma loka, also called *satya loka*, the realm of Brahma or truth, is the place where we can achieve freedom from the cycles of unrest. In this highest abode of creation, a mystical river named *Virajanadi* is supposed to give shelter to living entities. One can see the reflection in the mirror clearly only when the mirror is clean. Similarly on the earth plane, if our mind is calm and pure, we can realise *Brahman*. When we leave this body, we cannot realise *Bramhan*. It is only in *Brahma loka* that we are never separated from him. In this plane, he can be seen as clearly as light and shade. This physical plane is where we should strive to know him.

70. SATTVA GUNA

Sattva guna is one of the three basic qualities inherent in a human being. *Sattva guna* brings stability and balance in the body nurturing selflessness, truth, knowledge, peace, harmony, creativity and positivity. It is the essential quality that helps create a peaceful and meaningful way of life.

71. *RAJO GUNA*

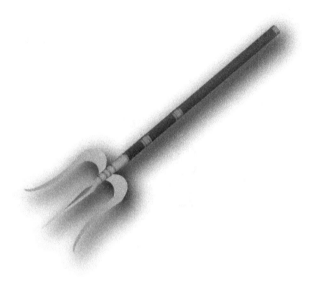

Rajo guna is also a basic quality that can manifest in an individual as tendencies of restlessness, constant activity and ambition. If the quality of *rajas* dominates an individual, they tend to gravitate towards material attachments. Although *rajas* is required, an excess of it can lead to anxiety, overthinking, aggressiveness and hyperactivity.

72. *TAMO GUNA*

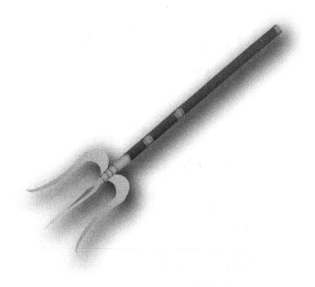

Tamo guna is another basic quality that is inherent within us. When it is out of balance, it can hamper a person's ability to gain higher consciousness and discover the unity of life. It is translated as darkness, illusion and ignorance. An excess of *tamo guna* causes inertia, lethargy, dullness and greed. When tamo *guna predominates*, people tend to procrastinate, sleep too much and neglect their responsibilities.

THE SNAKES ON
THE BOARD

Irshya (12) **leads to** *Trishna* (8) – Jealousy always leads to greed, poverty and suffering. If one is content with what one has, it is easy to be peaceful. Comparing yourself to others can create a constant loop of craving.

Dvesha (16) **leads to** *Lobha* (4) – *Dvesha* is intense hatred, which comes from a sense of limitation. It is stored deep in the subconscious mind. *Dvesha* takes one to *lobha*. Insecurity can make one hoard things and indulge excessively in material pleasures.

Dusang (24) **leads to** *Mada* (7) – *Dusanga* or bad company can pull a person down to *mada*, a kind of intoxication. To come out of this state, you need to be aware of who is bad company.

Adharm (29) **leads to** *Moha* (6) – Doing *adharmic* activities can give you compulsive desires. When you fall into a state of *moha*, your *budhi* (intelligence) is compromised.

Avidya (**29**) **leads to** *Kama* (**6**) – Lack of intelligence lands you in lust. The mind limits and thinks it has complete knowledge. *Avidya* is a lack of complete intelligence. When one is unable to see a situation from different angles, actions become limited. *Kama* should be acknowledged and fulfilled in a balanced way. When *kama* supports *dharma*, it is healthy.

Himsa (**52**) **leads to** *Narak* (**35**) – Violence in thought or action towards others constitutes *himsa*. The snake shows that you have impure actions and thoughts. Calm your thoughts at every single step.

Ahankar (**55**) **leads to** *Maya* (**2**) – If someone gives you something valuable, you may push it away. *Ahankar* is a tendency to think of oneself as greater than others. Such a person uses words and actions in a demeaning way. It will pull you down to *maya* and make you think everything is fine.

Durbudhi (**61**) **leads to** *Antariksha* (**6**) – The intellect should be used for constructive purposes to elevate yourself. Lack of a refined intellect will harm other people and lead you to *antariksha*, a sort of non-man's sphere, a space between worlds, where you are lost. If you can elevate *durbudhi* and turn it to *satbudhi*, for example by engaging in *satsanga* or doing charity, you can turn things around.

Tamas (**63**) **leads to** *Krodh* (**3**) – Time does not wait for anyone. *Tamasic* tendencies will not help you survive anywhere in the world. Observe whether other people's progress creates *krodha* in you. You may have tremendous anger and rage. You tend to dwell in the past.

Tamo Guna (72) leads to Prithvi (51) – *Tamo guna* causes you to fall back to *Prithvi*. You come back to the elemental composition of the earth plane. You have to balance all five elements once again to have physical and mental health. When you have an excess of *tamo guna*, you have fatigue, you feel less confident and less tolerant. The *Prithvi mudra* can help you boost your self-confidence. All the *gunas* are required to exist on the earth plane, but you need to balance them.

LADDERS ON
THE BOARD

***Tapasya* (10) to *Swarg* (23)** – When karmic patterns are burned through meditation and *tapasya*, you can rise to the next level of heaven.

***Daya* (17) to *Brahma loka* (69)** – When you discover your innate *daya*, you can change your destiny. This will lead you to the zone of creation. *Daya* is sensitivity to others. It means compassion and empathy not only for fellow humans but also animals, plants and the earth.

***Daan* (20) to *Mahar loka* (32)** – The spirit of *daan* allows you to raise your frequency and move very fast in this plane.

***Dharma* (22) to *Satbudhi* (60)** – Abiding by *dharma* gives you the highest intelligence.

***Paramdharma* (27) to *Jan loka* (41)** – Observing the highest *dharma* without any expectation takes you to a higher human plane.

Swadharma (28) to *Satyalok* (59) – Righteous thought and action combined with faith and trust give you the ability to reach *satya loka*, the plane of truth.

Gyan (37) to *Ananda Loka* (66) – Acquiring hidden knowledge that you cannot obtain from books takes you to the plane of bliss.

Suvidya (45) to *Shiva Loka* (67) – Acquiring supreme hidden divine knowledge within transports you to the dimension of *Shiva loka*.

Viveka (46) to *Sukh* (62) – Discrimination in thought produces good words. The control of breath and action leads to peace and happiness.

Bhakti (54) to *Vaikunth Loka* (68) – Devotion and surrender take you to a blemish-free world. Bhakti cannot be measured or described in ordinary words.